My
WORRY
journal

DATE TODAY:................. M T W T F S S

WORRY OF THE DAY:

_____
_____
_____
_____
_____
_____

HOW WORRIED
ARE YOU?

 10

RATE OUT OF 10!

Doodle/ Stick/ Draw About Your Worry
Here:

Is There someone you can talk to about it?

WHEN WILL YOU TALK TO THEM? _____

3 Little Ideas - That Could Help!

1 _____

2 _____

3 _____

Extra notes: _____
_____
_____
_____
_____
_____
_____

DATE TODAY:................. M T W T F S S

WORRY OF THE DAY:

_____

_____

_____

_____

_____

_____

_____

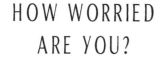 HOW WORRIED
ARE YOU? **10** RATE OUT OF 10!

Doodle/ Stick/ Draw About Your Worry
Here:

Is There someone you can talk to about it?

WHEN WILL YOU TALK TO THEM? _____

3 little Ideas - That Could Help!

1 _____

2 _____

3 _____

Extra notes: _____
_____
_____
_____
_____
_____
_____
_____

DATE TODAY:................. M T W T F S S

WORRY OF THE DAY:

_____

_____

_____

_____

_____

_____

_____

HOW WORRIED
ARE YOU?

 10

RATE OUT OF 10!

Doodle/ Stick/ Draw About Your Worry
Here:

Is There someone you can talk to about it?

WHEN WILL YOU TALK TO THEM? _____

3 Little Ideas - That Could Help!

1 _____

2 _____

3 _____

Extra notes:

_____
_____
_____
_____
_____
_____

DATE TODAY:................. M T W T F S S

WORRY OF THE DAY:

_____
_____
_____
_____
_____
_____

HOW WORRIED
ARE YOU?

RATE OUT OF 10!

Doodle/ Stick/ Draw About Your Worry
Here:

Is There someone you can talk to about it?

WHEN WILL YOU TALK TO THEM? _____

3 Little Ideas - That Could Help!

1 _____

2 _____

3 _____

Extra notes: _____

_____

_____

_____

_____

_____

_____

_____

DATE TODAY:................. M T W T F S S

WORRY OF THE DAY:

_____

_____

_____

_____

_____

_____

_____

HOW WORRIED RATE OUT OF 10!
ARE YOU?

Doodle/ Stick/ Draw About Your Worry
Here:

Is There someone you can talk to about it?

WHEN WILL YOU TALK TO THEM? _____

3 Little Ideas - That Could Help!

1 _____

2 _____

3 _____

Extra notes:

WORRY OF THE DAY:

_____

_____

_____

_____

_____

_____

_____

HOW WORRIED ARE YOU?   RATE OUT OF 10!

Doodle/ Stick/ Draw About Your Worry Here:

Is There someone you can talk to about it?

WHEN WILL YOU TALK TO THEM? _____

3 Little Ideas - That Could Help!

1. _____
2. _____
3. _____

Extra notes: _____
_____
_____
_____
_____
_____
_____

DATE TODAY:.................. M T W T F S S

WORRY OF THE DAY:

_____

_____

_____

_____

_____

_____

HOW WORRIED
ARE YOU?

RATE OUT OF 10!

Doodle/ Stick/ Draw About Your Worry
Here:

Is There someone you can talk to about it?

WHEN WILL YOU TALK TO THEM? _____

3 little Ideas - That Could Help!

1 _____

2 _____

3 _____

Extra notes: _____
_____
_____
_____
_____
_____
_____

WORRY OF THE DAY:

_____
_____
_____
_____
_____
_____

 HOW WORRIED ARE YOU? $\overline{10}$ RATE OUT OF 10!

Doodle/ Stick/ Draw About Your Worry Here:

Is There someone you can talk to about it?

WHEN WILL YOU TALK TO THEM? _____

3 Little Ideas - That Could Help!

1 _____

2 _____

3 _____

Extra notes: _____
_____
_____
_____
_____
_____
_____
_____

WORRY OF THE DAY:

_____
_____
_____
_____
_____
_____
_____

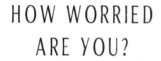 HOW WORRIED ARE YOU?   10 RATE OUT OF 10!

Doodle/ Stick/ Draw About Your Worry Here:

Is There someone you can talk to about it?

WHEN WILL YOU TALK TO THEM? _____

3 Little Ideas - That Could Help!

1 _____

2 _____

3 _____

Extra notes:
_____
_____
_____
_____
_____
_____
_____

DATE TODAY:................. M T W T F S S

WORRY OF THE DAY:

_____

_____

_____

_____

_____

_____

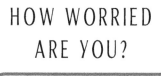 HOW WORRIED ARE YOU?

 10

RATE OUT OF 10!

Doodle/ Stick/ Draw About Your Worry Here:

Is There someone you can talk to about it?

WHEN WILL YOU TALK TO THEM? _____

3 Little Ideas - That Could Help!

1 _____

2 _____

3 _____

Extra notes:
_____
_____
_____
_____
_____
_____
_____

DATE TODAY:................. M T W T F S S

WORRY OF THE DAY:

_____
_____
_____
_____
_____
_____
_____

HOW WORRIED
ARE YOU?

 10

RATE OUT OF 10!

Doodle/ Stick/ Draw About Your Worry
Here:

Is There someone you can talk to about it?

WHEN WILL YOU TALK TO THEM? _____

3 Little Ideas - That Could Help!

1 _____

2 _____

3 _____

Extra notes: _____

_____

_____

_____

_____

_____

_____

_____

DATE TODAY:................ M T W T F S S

WORRY OF THE DAY:

_____
_____
_____
_____
_____
_____
_____

HOW WORRIED
ARE YOU?

$\dfrac{}{10}$

RATE OUT OF 10!

Doodle/ Stick/ Draw About Your Worry
Here:

Is There someone you can talk to about it?

WHEN WILL YOU TALK TO THEM? _____

3 Little Ideas - That Could Help!

1 _____

2 _____

3 _____

Extra notes:
_____
_____
_____
_____
_____
_____
_____

DATE TODAY:................. M T W T F S S

WORRY OF THE DAY:

_____

_____

_____

_____

_____

_____

_____

HOW WORRIED
ARE YOU?

10

RATE OUT OF 10!

Doodle/ Stick/ Draw About Your Worry
Here:

Is There someone you can talk to about it?

WHEN WILL YOU TALK TO THEM? _____

3 Little Ideas - That Could Help!

1 _____

2 _____

3 _____

Extra notes:

WORRY OF THE DAY:

HOW WORRIED
ARE YOU?

 10

RATE OUT OF 10!

Doodle/ Stick/ Draw About Your Worry
Here:

Is There someone you can talk to about it?

WHEN WILL YOU TALK TO THEM? _____

3 Little Ideas - That Could Help!

1 _____

2 _____

3 _____

Extra notes: _____
_____
_____
_____
_____
_____
_____
_____

DATE TODAY:................. M T W T F S S

WORRY OF THE DAY:

_____

_____

_____

_____

_____

_____

_____

HOW WORRIED
ARE YOU?

RATE OUT OF 10!

Doodle/ Stick/ Draw About Your Worry
Here:

Is There someone you can talk to about it?

WHEN WILL YOU TALK TO THEM? _____

3 Little Ideas - That Could Help!

1 _____

2 _____

3 _____

Extra notes: _____
_____
_____
_____
_____
_____
_____

DATE TODAY:................ M T W T F S S

WORRY OF THE DAY:

_____

_____

_____

_____

_____

_____

HOW WORRIED
ARE YOU?

$\frac{\quad}{10}$

RATE OUT OF 10!

Doodle/ Stick/ Draw About Your Worry
Here:

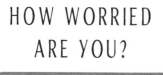

Is There someone you can talk to about it?

WHEN WILL YOU TALK TO THEM? _____

3 Little Ideas - That Could Help!

1 _____

2 _____

3 _____

Extra notes: _____
_____
_____
_____
_____
_____
_____
_____

DATE TODAY:................ M T W T F S S

WORRY OF THE DAY:

_____

_____

_____

_____

_____

_____

_____

HOW WORRIED
ARE YOU?

10
RATE OUT OF 10!

Doodle/ Stick/ Draw About Your Worry
Here:

Is There someone you can talk to about it?

→

WHEN WILL YOU TALK TO THEM? _____

3 Little Ideas - That Could Help!

1 _____

2 _____

3 _____

Extra notes: _____
_____
_____
_____
_____
_____
_____

DATE TODAY:................. M T W T F S S

WORRY OF THE DAY:

_____
_____
_____
_____
_____
_____
_____

HOW WORRIED
ARE YOU?

 10

RATE OUT OF 10!

Doodle/ Stick/ Draw About Your Worry
Here:

Is There someone you can talk to about it?

WHEN WILL YOU TALK TO THEM? _____

3 Little Ideas - That Could Help!

1 _____

2 _____

3 _____

Extra notes: _____
_____
_____
_____
_____
_____
_____

DATE TODAY:................ M T W T F S S

WORRY OF THE DAY:

_____

_____

_____

_____

_____

_____

HOW WORRIED
ARE YOU?

10

RATE OUT OF 10!

Doodle/ Stick/ Draw About Your Worry
Here:

Is There someone you can talk to about it?

WHEN WILL YOU TALK TO THEM? _____

3 Little Ideas - That Could Help!

1 _____

2 _____

3 _____

Extra notes: _____
_____
_____
_____
_____
_____
_____
_____

DATE TODAY:................ M T W T F S S

WORRY OF THE DAY:

_____

_____

_____

_____

_____

_____

_____

HOW WORRIED
ARE YOU?

 10

RATE OUT OF 10!

Doodle/ Stick/ Draw About Your Worry
Here:

Is There someone you can talk to about it?

WHEN WILL YOU TALK TO THEM? _____

3 Little Ideas - That Could Help!

1 _____

2 _____

3 _____

Extra notes: _____
_____
_____
_____
_____
_____
_____

DATE TODAY:................. M T W T F S S

WORRY OF THE DAY:

_____
_____
_____
_____
_____
_____
_____

HOW WORRIED
ARE YOU?

10

RATE OUT OF 10!

Doodle/ Stick/ Draw About Your Worry
Here:

Is There someone you can talk to about it?

WHEN WILL YOU TALK TO THEM? _____

3 Little Ideas - That Could Help!

1 _____

2 _____

3 _____

Extra notes:
_____
_____
_____
_____
_____
_____

DATE TODAY:................ M T W T F S S

WORRY OF THE DAY:

_____
_____
_____
_____
_____
_____

_____

HOW WORRIED
ARE YOU?

 10

RATE OUT OF 10!

Doodle/ Stick/ Draw About Your Worry
Here:

Is There someone you can talk to about it?

WHEN WILL YOU TALK TO THEM? _____

3 Little Ideas - That Could Help!

1 _____

2 _____

3 _____

Extra notes: _____
_____
_____
_____
_____
_____
_____

WORRY OF THE DAY:

HOW WORRIED
ARE YOU?

 $\frac{\quad}{10}$

RATE OUT OF 10!

Doodle/ Stick/ Draw About Your Worry
Here:

Is There someone you can talk to about it?

WHEN WILL YOU TALK TO THEM? _____

3 Little Ideas - That Could Help!

1 _____

2 _____

3 _____

Extra notes: _____

_____

_____

_____

_____

_____

_____

_____

WORRY OF THE DAY:

_____

_____

_____

_____

_____

_____

_____

HOW WORRIED ARE YOU?

RATE OUT OF 10!

Doodle/ Stick/ Draw About Your Worry Here:

Is There someone you can talk to about it?

WHEN WILL YOU TALK TO THEM? _____

3 Little Ideas - That Could Help!

1 _____

2 _____

3 _____

Extra notes: _____
_____
_____
_____
_____
_____
_____

DATE TODAY:................. M T W T F S S

WORRY OF THE DAY:

_____

_____

_____

_____

_____

HOW WORRIED
ARE YOU? RATE OUT OF 10!

Doodle/ Stick/ Draw About Your Worry
Here:

Is There someone you can talk to about it?

WHEN WILL YOU TALK TO THEM? _____

3 Little Ideas - That Could Help!

1. _____

2. _____

3. _____

Extra notes: _____
_____
_____
_____
_____
_____
_____

DATE TODAY:................. M T W T F S S

WORRY OF THE DAY:

_____

_____

_____

_____

_____

_____

_____

 HOW WORRIED
ARE YOU? RATE OUT OF 10!

Doodle/ Stick/ Draw About Your Worry
Here:

Is There someone you can talk to about it?

WHEN WILL YOU TALK TO THEM? _____

3 Little Ideas - That Could Help!

1 _____

2 _____

3 _____

Extra notes: _____
_____
_____
_____
_____
_____
_____
_____

WORRY OF THE DAY:

_____

_____

_____

_____

_____

_____

_____

HOW WORRIED
ARE YOU?

RATE OUT OF 10!

Doodle/ Stick/ Draw About Your Worry
Here:

Is There someone you can talk to about it?

WHEN WILL YOU TALK TO THEM? _____

3 Little Ideas - That Could Help!

1. _____

2. _____

3. _____

Extra notes: _____
_____
_____
_____
_____
_____
_____

DATE TODAY:................. M T W T F S S

WORRY OF THE DAY:

_____

_____

_____

_____

_____

_____

HOW WORRIED
ARE YOU?  RATE OUT OF 10!

Doodle/ Stick/ Draw About Your Worry
Here:

Is There someone you can talk to about it?

WHEN WILL YOU TALK TO THEM? _____

3 Little Ideas - That Could Help!

1 _____

2 _____

3 _____

Extra notes: _____
_____
_____
_____
_____
_____
_____

DATE TODAY:................. M T W T F S S

WORRY OF THE DAY:

_____

_____

_____

_____

_____

_____

_____

HOW WORRIED
ARE YOU? RATE OUT OF 10!

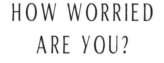

Doodle/ Stick/ Draw About Your Worry
Here:

Is There someone you can talk to about it?

WHEN WILL YOU TALK TO THEM? _____

3 Little Ideas - That Could Help!

1 _____

2 _____

3 _____

Extra notes:
_____
_____
_____
_____
_____
_____
_____

DATE TODAY:................ M T W T F S S

WORRY OF THE DAY:

_____

_____

_____

_____

_____

_____

HOW WORRIED ARE YOU?   RATE OUT OF 10!

Doodle/ Stick/ Draw About Your Worry Here:

Is There someone you can talk to about it?

WHEN WILL YOU TALK TO THEM? _____

3 Little Ideas - That Could Help!

1 _____

2 _____

3 _____

Extra notes: _____
_____
_____
_____
_____
_____
_____

DATE TODAY:................. M T W T F S S

WORRY OF THE DAY:

_____

_____

_____

_____

_____

_____

 HOW WORRIED ARE YOU? RATE OUT OF 10!

Doodle/ Stick/ Draw About Your Worry Here:

Is There someone you can talk to about it?

WHEN WILL YOU TALK TO THEM? _____

3 Little Ideas - That Could Help!

1 _____

2 _____

3 _____

Extra notes:
_____
_____
_____
_____
_____
_____
_____

WORRY OF THE DAY:

_____

_____

_____

_____

_____

_____

_____

HOW WORRIED ARE YOU? RATE OUT OF 10!

Doodle/ Stick/ Draw About Your Worry Here:

Is There someone you can talk to about it?

WHEN WILL YOU TALK TO THEM? _____

3 Little Ideas - That Could Help!

1 _____

2 _____

3 _____

Extra notes: _____
_____
_____
_____
_____
_____
_____

WORRY OF THE DAY:

_____

_____

_____

_____

_____

_____

_____

HOW WORRIED ARE YOU?

 RATE OUT OF 10!

Doodle/ Stick/ Draw About Your Worry Here:

Is There someone you can talk to about it?

WHEN WILL YOU TALK TO THEM? _____

3 Little Ideas - That Could Help!

1 _____

2 _____

3 _____

Extra notes: _____
_____
_____
_____
_____
_____
_____
_____

WORRY OF THE DAY:

_____

_____

_____

_____

_____

_____

HOW WORRIED
ARE YOU?

10

RATE OUT OF 10!

Doodle/ Stick/ Draw About Your Worry
Here:

Is There someone you can talk to about it?

WHEN WILL YOU TALK TO THEM? _____

3 Little Ideas - That Could Help!

1 _____

2 _____

3 _____

Extra notes:

DATE TODAY:................ M T W T F S S

WORRY OF THE DAY:

_____
_____
_____
_____
_____
_____
_____

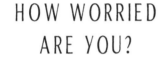 HOW WORRIED ARE YOU? RATE OUT OF 10!

Doodle/ Stick/ Draw About Your Worry Here:

Is There someone you can talk to about it?

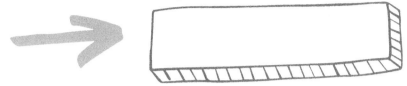

WHEN WILL YOU TALK TO THEM? _____

3 Little Ideas - That Could Help!

1 _____

2 _____

3 _____

Extra notes:
_____
_____
_____
_____
_____
_____
_____

WORRY OF THE DAY:

_____
_____
_____
_____
_____
_____

 HOW WORRIED ARE YOU?

 $\frac{\ }{10}$ RATE OUT OF 10!

Doodle/ Stick/ Draw About Your Worry Here:

Is There someone you can talk to about it?

WHEN WILL YOU TALK TO THEM? _____

3 Little Ideas - That Could Help!

1 _____

2 _____

3 _____

Extra notes:
_____
_____
_____
_____
_____
_____
_____

DATE TODAY:................. M T W T F S S

WORRY OF THE DAY:

_____

_____

_____

_____

_____

_____

_____

HOW WORRIED
ARE YOU?

10

RATE OUT OF 10!

Doodle/ Stick/ Draw About Your Worry
Here:

Is There someone you can talk to about it?

WHEN WILL YOU TALK TO THEM? _____

3 Little Ideas - That Could Help!

1 _____

2 _____

3 _____

Extra notes: _____
_____
_____
_____
_____
_____
_____
_____

WORRY OF THE DAY:

_____

_____

_____

_____

_____

_____

 HOW WORRIED ARE YOU? **10** RATE OUT OF 10!

Doodle/ Stick/ Draw About Your Worry Here:

Is There someone you can talk to about it?

WHEN WILL YOU TALK TO THEM? _____

3 Little Ideas - That Could Help!

1 _____

2 _____

3 _____

Extra notes: _____
_____
_____
_____
_____
_____
_____
_____

DATE TODAY:................ M T W T F S S

WORRY OF THE DAY:

_____

_____

_____

_____

_____

_____

_____

HOW WORRIED
ARE YOU?

 RATE OUT OF 10!

Doodle/ Stick/ Draw About Your Worry
Here:

Is There someone you can talk to about it?

WHEN WILL YOU TALK TO THEM? _____

3 Little Ideas - That Could Help!

1 _____

2 _____

3 _____

Extra notes: _____
_____
_____
_____
_____
_____
_____

DATE TODAY:................. M T W T F S S

WORRY OF THE DAY:

_____

_____

_____

_____

_____

_____

HOW WORRIED
ARE YOU? RATE OUT OF 10!

$\dfrac{\quad}{10}$

Doodle/ Stick/ Draw About Your Worry
Here:

Is There someone you can talk to about it?

WHEN WILL YOU TALK TO THEM? _____

3 Little Ideas - That Could Help!

1 _____

2 _____

3 _____

Extra notes: _____
_____
_____
_____
_____
_____
_____
_____

DATE TODAY:................. M T W T F S S

WORRY OF THE DAY:

_____

_____

_____

_____

_____

_____

HOW WORRIED ARE YOU? RATE OUT OF 10!

Doodle/ Stick/ Draw About Your Worry Here:

Is There someone you can talk to about it?

WHEN WILL YOU TALK TO THEM? _____

3 Little Ideas - That Could Help!

1 _____

2 _____

3 _____

Extra notes: _____
_____
_____
_____
_____
_____
_____

WORRY OF THE DAY:

_____

_____

_____

_____

_____

_____

 HOW WORRIED ARE YOU? RATE OUT OF 10!

Doodle/ Stick/ Draw About Your Worry Here:

Is There someone you can talk to about it?

WHEN WILL YOU TALK TO THEM? _____

3 Little Ideas - That Could Help!

1 _____

2 _____

3 _____

Extra notes: _____
_____
_____
_____
_____
_____
_____

DATE TODAY:................. M T W T F S S

WORRY OF THE DAY:

_____
_____
_____
_____
_____
_____

HOW WORRIED
ARE YOU?

RATE OUT OF 10!

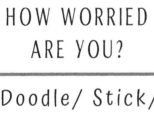

Doodle/ Stick/ Draw About Your Worry
Here:

Is There someone you can talk to about it?

WHEN WILL YOU TALK TO THEM? _____

3 Little Ideas - That Could Help!

1 _____

2 _____

3 _____

Extra notes:
_____
_____
_____
_____
_____
_____
_____

WORRY OF THE DAY:

_____
_____
_____
_____
_____
_____

HOW WORRIED ARE YOU?

 10 RATE OUT OF 10!

Doodle/ Stick/ Draw About Your Worry Here:

Is There someone you can talk to about it?

WHEN WILL YOU TALK TO THEM? _____

3 Little Ideas - That Could Help!

1 _____

2 _____

3 _____

Extra notes: _____
_____
_____
_____
_____
_____
_____

DATE TODAY:................. M T W T F S S

WORRY OF THE DAY:

_____

_____

_____

_____

_____

_____

HOW WORRIED
ARE YOU?

RATE OUT OF 10!

Doodle/ Stick/ Draw About Your Worry
Here:

Is There someone you can talk to about it?

WHEN WILL YOU TALK TO THEM? _____

3 Little Ideas - That Could Help!

1. _____
2. _____
3. _____

Extra notes:
_____
_____
_____
_____
_____
_____

DATE TODAY:................. M T W T F S S

WORRY OF THE DAY:

_____

_____

_____

_____

_____

_____

HOW WORRIED
ARE YOU?

10

RATE OUT OF 10!

Doodle/ Stick/ Draw About Your Worry
Here:

Is There someone you can talk to about it?

WHEN WILL YOU TALK TO THEM? _____

3 Little Ideas - That Could Help!

1 _____

2 _____

3 _____

Extra notes: _____
_____
_____
_____
_____
_____
_____

DATE TODAY:................. M T W T F S S

WORRY OF THE DAY:

_____

_____

_____

_____

_____

_____

_____

HOW WORRIED
ARE YOU?   RATE OUT OF 10!

Doodle/ Stick/ Draw About Your Worry
Here:

Is There someone you can talk to about it?

WHEN WILL YOU TALK TO THEM? _____

3 Little Ideas - That Could Help!

1 _____

2 _____

3 _____

Extra notes: _____
_____
_____
_____
_____
_____
_____

DATE TODAY:................. M T W T F S S

WORRY OF THE DAY:

_____

_____

_____

_____

_____

_____

_____

HOW WORRIED
ARE YOU?

 10

RATE OUT OF 10!

Doodle/ Stick/ Draw About Your Worry
Here:

Is There someone you can talk to about it?

WHEN WILL YOU TALK TO THEM? _____

3 Little Ideas - That Could Help!

1 _____

2 _____

3 _____

Extra notes: _____
_____
_____
_____
_____
_____
_____
_____

DATE TODAY:................. M T W T F S S

WORRY OF THE DAY:

_____

_____

_____

_____

_____

_____

HOW WORRIED
ARE YOU?

10

RATE OUT OF 10!

Doodle/ Stick/ Draw About Your Worry
Here:

Is There someone you can talk to about it?

WHEN WILL YOU TALK TO THEM? _____

3 Little Ideas - That Could Help!

1 _____

2 _____

3 _____

Extra notes:
_____
_____
_____
_____
_____
_____
_____

DATE TODAY:................. M T W T F S S

WORRY OF THE DAY:

_____

_____

_____

_____

_____

_____

_____

HOW WORRIED
ARE YOU?

RATE OUT OF 10!

Doodle/ Stick/ Draw About Your Worry
Here:

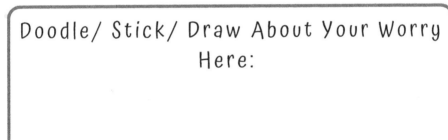

Is There someone you can talk to about it?

WHEN WILL YOU TALK TO THEM? _____

3 Little Ideas - That Could Help!

1 _____

2 _____

3 _____

Extra notes: _____
_____
_____
_____
_____
_____
_____

DATE TODAY:................. M T W T F S S

WORRY OF THE DAY:

_____

_____

_____

_____

_____

_____

_____

HOW WORRIED
ARE YOU?

RATE OUT OF 10!

Doodle/ Stick/ Draw About Your Worry
Here:

Is There someone you can talk to about it?

WHEN WILL YOU TALK TO THEM? _____

3 Little Ideas - That Could Help!

1 _____

2 _____

3 _____

Extra notes:
_____
_____
_____
_____
_____
_____
_____

DATE TODAY:................ M T W T F S S

WORRY OF THE DAY:

_____

_____

_____

_____

_____

_____

HOW WORRIED
ARE YOU?

10

RATE OUT OF 10!

Doodle/ Stick/ Draw About Your Worry
Here:

Is There someone you can talk to about it?

WHEN WILL YOU TALK TO THEM? _____

3 Little Ideas - That Could Help!

1 _____

2 _____

3 _____

Extra notes: _____
_____
_____
_____
_____
_____
_____

WORRY OF THE DAY:

_____
_____
_____
_____
_____
_____

_____

HOW WORRIED
ARE YOU?

RATE OUT OF 10!

Doodle/ Stick/ Draw About Your Worry
Here:

Is There someone you can talk to about it?

WHEN WILL YOU TALK TO THEM? _____

3 Little Ideas - That Could Help!

1 _____

2 _____

3 _____

Extra notes: _____
_____
_____
_____
_____
_____
_____